THE
WISDOM OF
CORMAC

W0081381

Leadership
Principles from
ANCIENT
IRELAND

Translated by
KUNO MEYER

ixia
PRESS

Mineola, New York

Bibliographical Note

This Ixia Press edition, first published in 2020, is a slightly abridged republication of *The Instructions of King Cormac Mac Airt*, originally published in 1909 as Volume XV in the Royal Irish Academy Todd Lecture Series by Hodges, Figgis, & Company, Ltd., Dublin, and Williams & Norgate, London.

Library of Congress Cataloging-in-Publication Data

Names: Cormac Mac Airt, King of Ireland, active 227-260. | Meyer, Kuno, 1858-1919, editor and translator. | Meyer, Kuno, 1858-1919 translator.
Title: The wisdom of Cormac : leadership principles from ancient Ireland / Translated by Kuno Meyer.
Other titles: Tecosca Cormaic.
Description: Mineola, New York : Dover Publications, Inc., 2020. | "This Dover edition, first published in 2020, is a slightly abridged republication of The instructions of King Cormac Mac Airt, originally published in 1909 as Volume VX in the Royal Irish Academy Todd Lecture Series by Hodges, Figgis, & Company, Ltd., Dublin, and Williams & Norgate, London." | Summary: "Cormaic Mac Airt, a third-century high king of Ireland, ruled during a time of prosperity and is revered for his wisdom and generosity. This set of his instructions, presented in a question-and-answer dialogue between the king and his son, offers advice on how to live an honest, respectable, and successful life—a blueprint from ancient Ireland that has universal resonance for modern readers"—Provided by publisher.
Identifiers: LCCN 2019040570 | ISBN 9780486842110 (trade paperback)
Subjects: LCSH: Maxims, Irish—Translations into English. | Proverbs, Irish—Translations into English. | Kings and rulers—Duties—Early works to 1800. | Cormac Mac Airt, King of Ireland, active 227-260. | Maxims, Irish.
Classification: LCC PB1421 .T43 2020 | DDC 398.9/9162—dc23
LC record available at https://lccn.loc.gov/2019040570

IXIA PRESS
An imprint of Dover Publications, Inc.

Manufactured in the United States by LSC Communications
84211801
www.doverpublications.com/ixiapress

2 4 6 8 10 9 7 5 3 1
2020

PREFACE

Among the gnomic literature of ancient Ireland, the instructions given by princes to their heirs, by tutors to their disciples, or by foster-fathers to their sons form a group by themselves. The oldest among them are those ascribed to Morann mac Móin, addressed to his foster-son Nére to be delivered by him to King Feradach Findfechtnach, who, according to the Annals of the Four Masters, was King of Ireland from 15 to 36 A.D. They are known as *Audacht, Auraicept,* or *Tecosc Morainn* 'The Bequest, Precept, or Instruction of Morann,' and to judge from their language were composed early in the eighth century. They have never been edited or translated.[1]

The Instructions of Cúchulaind to his foster-son Lugaid of the Red Stripes, known as *Briatharthecosc Conculaind,* form an episode in the tale called the 'Sickbed of Cúchulaind,' edited by Windisch in his *Irische Texte,* vol. I, p. 213-214. They have often been translated, by O'Curry in *Atlantis,* vol. I, pp. 362-392, and vol. II, pp. 98-124; by Brian O'Looney in the *Facsimiles of the*

---

1   For an enumeration of the MSS. in which this text has come down to us, see D'Arbois de Jubainville's *Catalogue,* p. 41, and add: Additional 33, 993 (British Museum), a fifteenth-century vellum, fo. 76-8 a. This is a fragment beginning: *Incipit auraicept Morainn nó tecusc Morainn for Feradach finnfechtnach. Comerig a Neire nuallgnaith noithiut buaid ngaire*; and breaking off abruptly with the words: *dligid beos cach dotche miscais dligid cach gúbrethach gaire.* As to the age of *Auraicept Morainn* see Strachan's note in his 'Deponent Verb,' p. 50.

In the Laws sets of legal maxims are ascribed to Morann. See vol. iv, p. 384.

National MSS. of Ireland; by D'Arbois de Jubainville in *L'Épopée celtique en Irlande*, pp. 186 -191; and by Miss E. Hull in her *Cuchullin Saga*, pp. 231-234.

A third collection of precepts and wise sayings is ascribed to the poet Fíthel or Fíthal, who is said to have lived at the court of King Cormac mac Airt in the third century. They are addressed to his son, and are known as *Senbríathra* or *Senráite Fíthail*.[2] Some of them are in the form of question and answer, like *Tecosca Cormaic*, a circumstance which has led many scribes to a confusion of the two. They have never been edited or translated; but some extracts from them will be found in Hardiman's *Minstrelsy*, vol. II, p. 396. Like *Tecosca Cormaic*, I would ascribe them to the ninth century.

Certain sayings of Fíthel are in some MSS. attributed to Flann Fína mac Ossu, by which name Aldfrid the son of king Osuiu (Oswy) of Northumberland was known in Ireland. Thus the strings of proverbs beginning respectively *Atchota soichell saidbrius*, *Ba faitech ar ná ba fíachach*, *Descaid cotulta freslige*, *Tosach eoluis imchomarc*, *Ferr dán orba* are ascribed to him in 23 N 10. and 23 D 2. Both these MSS. also attribute to him a number of sayings which begin like § 15 of my edition of *Tecosca Cormaic*, but continue *Dligid fír fortacht, dligid gó a cairiugud*, &c. Under the heading *Flann Fína beos* 23 D 2 further assigns to him the following interesting piece, which, as I have never come across it in any other manuscript, I will print and translate *in extenso*:—

Cia féighe rángais? Fir Mhuighi Féine 7 gaoth.

Cia hannsa rángais? Araidh Cliach 7 arc[h]oin.

---

2 See the MSS. enumerated in D'Arbois de Jubainville's *Catalogue*, p. 205. For a poetical dialogue between Fíthel and King Cormac see my *Hibernica Minora*, p. 82.

Cia solmha rángais? Osraighe 7 deamhnae.

Cia dána rángais? Corco Laeighde 7 . . . .

Cia tétem rángais? Na Déisi 7 miolchoin.

Cia heg*laige* rángais? Húi Líatháin 7 caoir*igh*.

Cia mesgamla rángais? Ciarraige 7 menntáin.

Cia húallcha rángais? Muscraigc 7 coil*igh* fedha.

Cia gairbe rángais? Orbraige 7 aitend.

Caite as dech rángais? A n-as[3] mesa do síol Aodha Sláine 7 a n-as[3] ferr díb-sein as fri hainglib nime at[4] cosmaile.

Cia mesamh rángais? A n-as deach Glasraighe 7 a 11-as mesa díb-sein as fri demnaibh at cosmaile.

"Who are the keenest you have met? The men of Mag Féne and wind.

Who are the most troublesome you have met? The Araid Cliach and watch-hounds.[5]

Who are the swiftest you have met? The men of Ossory and demons.

Who are the boldest you have met? The Corco Laeigde and . . . .

Who are the wantonest you have met? The Deissi and hounds.

Who are the most timid you have met? The Húi Liatháin and sheep.

Who are the most drunken you have met? The men of Kerry[6] and titmice.

Who are the proudest you have met? The men of Muskerry and wood-cocks.

---

3   inas MS.

4   ata MS.

5   Perhaps, *árchoin* 'slaughter-hounds.'

6   Perhaps one of the other districts anciently called Ciarraige is meant, such as Ciarraige Ai in co. Roscommon.

Who are the roughest you have met? The men of Orbraige[7] and furze.

Who are the best you have met? The worst part of the race of Aed Sláne;[8] and those who are best of them are like unto angels of Heaven.

Who are the worst you have met? The best part of the Glasraige;[9] and those who are worst of them are like unto demons."

In 23 N 27, p. 33, a set of sayings beginning *Maith dán ecna dogní rí[g] do bocht* is attributed to Flann Fíona mac Cosa(*sic*).

The 'Instructions of Cormac' have not before been published or translated in their entirety. A few selections from the text of the Book of Ballymote were translated by Hardiman l.c. O'Donovan's edition and translation from the Book of Lecan in the *Dublin Penny Journal* of December, 1832, and January, 1833, are well known; but the text which he followed is both incomplete and faulty, and his renderings can now be much improved upon. The following edition is based upon a comparison of all available MSS. which I will briefly characterize.

L, i.e. the Book of Leinster, a MS. of the twelfth century, pp. 343-345. In spite of its age and fine penmanship this MS. does not, as I have repeatedly pointed out, supply us with accurate and trustworthy texts. The copy of Tecosca Cormaic contained in it has many faulty readings,

---

7   The name of this tribe is preserved in that of the barony of Orrery, in co. Cork.

8   King of Ireland from 598-604.

9   In the *Triads* § 45 this tribe is mentioned as one of the three 'evils' or 'evil ones' of Ireland.

such as *ríglach* (p. 343*b*40) for *riaglach* (§ 3, 10), *ales*
(p. 343*b*21) for *ata lais* (§ 2, 24), *imtholta* (p. 345, 17)
for *imscoltad* (§ 22, 10), *cátingud* (ib. 25) for *cathugud*
(ib. 17), *éthech* (p. 345*c*) for *etech* (§ 31, 9), *trebar* (ib.)
for *trebad* (ib. 10), *forus* (ib.) for *árus* (ib. 11), *fuacht*
(ib.) for *fuchacht* or *fuichecht* (ib. 14) &c.

B, i.e. the Book of Ballymote, a MS. of the fourteenth
century, pp. 62*a*-65*a*. Like L, it mixes up *Tecosca
Cormaic* with *Bríathra Fíthail*, passing suddenly
from *Cormac dixit fri Coirpre* (p. 65*a*13) to *ol a mac fri
Fíthul* (ib. 32). The text, though good on the whole,
is never quite reliable, the scribe often blundering
in an almost incredible manner.[10] Several sections
are left out.

Lec, i.e. the Book of Lecan, a MS. of the fifteenth
century, fo. 420*a*-422*a*, and pp. 179-180 in the
codex H. 2. 17 (Trin. Coll.), with which some of
the leaves of the Book of Lecan are now bound up.
Neither a complete nor very accurate version.

N[1], i.e. the MS. marked 23 N 17 (R.I.A.) containing
in its vellum portion from p. 1-6 a large fragment
of our text.[11] A careful and copy on the whole.

N[2], i.e. the paper MS. marked 23 N 17 (R.I.A.) written
in 1714 by Domhnall ó Duind mac Eimuinn. Here

---

10   A warning instance of such blundering is to be found on
p. 37*d*32, where a sentence which stands correctly in LL. p. 354*b*
as follows: *Ruman mac Colmain in fili diata sil Rumain i nAth Truim.
Tri filid in domain .i. Homer ó Grécaib 7 Fergil ó Latinnaib et Ruman
ó Gœdelaib*, is made into: *Rumann mac Colmáin .i. poeta diada sil
Rumaind a nAth Truim .i. Hi Aenir oc Crœibh 7 Fergil o Laitrib.*

11   For a brief description of the MS. see *Eriu*, vol. I, p. 38, and *Triads of
Ireland*, p. vi.

on fo. 7*b-32b* is a carefully written and heavily glossed copy of the *Tecosca*. In 1828 O'Donovan made a transcript of it which, numbered 23 O 20, is preserved in the library of the Royal Irish Academy.

D, i.e. a small paper octavo marked 23 D 2 (R.I.A.). Though written in the seventeenth century it contains in a remarkably neat hand both the most complete and by far the best copy of the *Tecosca*.

H¹, i.e. the paper MS. numbered H. 1. 15 (Trin. Coll.), written in 1745 by Tadhg ua Neachtain. Under the title *Teagasg Riogh* it contains on pp. 149-174 a fairly complete and on the whole pretty accurate copy of our text.

H², i.e. the eighteenth-century paper manuscript numbered H. 1. 9. (Trin. Coll.) pp. 59 to the end, a poor copy, of which I have hardly made any use.

H³, i.e. the paper MS. numbered H. 4. 8. (Trin. Coll.), copied in the latter half of the seventeenth century by Dr. Joannes Beaton from a vellum manuscript. It once belonged to the Welsh antiquary Edward Lloyd, entries in English and Welsh by whom are found at the beginning of the volume. This copy also has so many defects that I have but rarely used it.

K, i.e. the sixteenth-century vellum marked VII., No. 3 in the Advocates' Library, Edinburgh. It contains from fo. 9a¹-9b² an imperfect, but fairly good copy of our text. It breaks off with § 18 of my edition.

Lastly, the paper MS. No. II among the Gaelic MSS. in the Advocates' Library in Edinburgh contains on ten pages an incomplete and faulty copy of our text written in the seventeenth century. I have not used it.[12] Nor have I thought it worth while to collate throughout a copy in the Book of Húi Maine, fo. 182a¹-182b, as it is identical with that of B.

I have already stated that N² is copiously glossed. Occasionally glosses are also found in B and in some of the other MSS. These glosses, like those of the Triads, were written at a time when Old-Irish was no longer understood, and are therefore of hardly any value. Besides, some of them are not explanatory, but etymological, such as *ilach* (§ 10, 4 in my edition) *.i. imat focul*. Many of them were collected for the purpose of forming a glossary of Old-Irish words,[13] and are to be found under the title *Incipit din Tecusc Rig budesta* in H. 3. 18, col. 539*a*. A few samples will characterise them sufficiently: — *argrinn goit* (§ 2, 8) *.i. tabach. airiti dála* (§ 6, 39) *.i. aentugud. turchomrac* (§ 3, 4) *.i. tinol. clandad dligid* (§ 2, 11) *.i. sadad nó cur. forsmaltaib* (§ 2, 21) *.i. caithem.*

---

12   I take this opportunity of saying that the copy of the *Triads* contained in the Kilbride MS. VII, No. 3 of the Edinburgh collection (not III, as stated in my Preface, p. vii), bears a close resemblance to the copies in the Book of Ballymote and in the Book of Húi Maine. A partial collation made by me yielded no important results. I have further found two fragments of the *Triads* in 23 N 7 (see above) fo. 1*a*-6*b*, beginning *ratha Laighnen* (§ 56), and ending *Cetheora aibghitre baoise baoithe condailbe imreasoin doingthe. FINIS.* and in C. 2. 3 (R.I.A.), a vellum MS. written in 1552, fo. 13*a*, beginning *Cend Eirenn Ardmacha*, and ending *tri scenb Hérenn Tulach na n-espoc Achadh Dea Duin m Buirigh* (§ 106), neither however of much importance.

13   As for the various stages in the preparation of alphabetical glossaries see *Archiv* iii, p. 138. That O'Clery made use of a collection of glosses on our text is shown by such items in his glossary as *atach ndroichbhérla* (§ 22, 5), *iomsgoltadh ngaoisi* (ib. 10), perhaps also *deithide* (§ 1, 6), *collach* (§ 15, 16), *goibhél* (§ 17, 7) &c.

foltaib (§ 2, 24) *.i. acra. athcomarc* (§ 3, 6) *.i. fiarfaide.*
diubairt (§ 3, 30) *.i. lethtrom. deide* (§ 1, 6) *senchasa .i.*
damachtain nó fulang. rob sobraid (§ 6, 4) *.i. soabraid. rop*
sognasaig[14] (§ 6, 17) *.i. gnai uais. tochus* (§ 6, 43) *.i. ealada.*
suilid (§ 7, 9) *.i. sofulaing. duilid* (§ 7, 10) *.i. dofulaing.*
meilcend (§ 7, 17) *.i. tabartus. cuire* (§ 8, 5) *.i. uir. riancobra*
(§ 11, 5) *.i. rianocobrach .i. saithech. teiti* (§ 10, 10) *.i. slighi.*
suanach (§ 13, 12) *.i. conaich. solom* (§ 13, 34) *.i. soluam.*
gabail (§ 14, 1) *.i. tinol ut dixit* (leg. dicitur) *Lebar Gabála.*
turrtugud (§ 14, 27) *.i. timpud. tirfochraic[215]* (§ 14, 27) *.i.*
cennach. toimdinach (§ 15, 2) *.i. dochusach. crinnach[316]* (§
15, 5) *.i. crin. disgir* (§ 15, 17) *.i. diaisc. itfaide* (§ 16, 17)
.i. saithech. resca (§ 16, 81) *.i. grasta. forcomat* (§ 16, 87) *.i.*
rogabat. faenbleogan (§ 16, 106) *.i. cendsugad*, &c.

Some of the glosses were evidently made on a text
occasionally differing from ours, e.g. *déide senchasa*
instead of *dethide senchasa* § 1, 6. Here *déitiu*, the O.-Ir.
verbal noun of *damur* or *daimim* (Middle-Ir. *daimthiu*), is
rightly glossed by *.i. damachtain no fulang.*

I think there can be no doubt that *Tecosca Cormaic* in
the form in which it has come down to us was compiled
during the Old-Irish period of the language, and, so far
as I can judge, not later than the first half of the ninth
century. The numerous verbal forms which it contains
seem to point to that time. The later forms of the infixed
pronouns which Strachan has pointed out in *Eriu* III, p.
158, such as *-das-* or *-dos-*, do not appear in our text.

---

14   The reading of L.
15   The reading of D N².
16   Instead of *crimnach*.

A tendency is occasionally apparent to link some of the lines of each paragraph together by alliteration in such a way that the initial sound of the last word in one line is repeated at the beginning of the next, e,g. § 14, 4:

> luge ria mbreith,
> bretha díana,
> dúscud ferge
> folabra gúach &c.

Professor O. J. Bergin and Dr. Whitley Stokes have had the kindness to read proofs of the text and translation, to point out mistakes and to suggest emendations, for which I desire to express my best thanks to them here.

K. M.

O grandson of Conn, O Cormac,' said Carbre, 'what is best for a king?'

'Not hard to tell,' said Cormac. 'Best for him

> Firmness without anger,
> Patience without strife,
> Affability without haughtiness,
> Taking care of ancient lore,
> Giving truth for truth,
> Hostages in fetters,
> Hosting with reason,
> Truth without addition,
> Mercifulness with consolation of law,
> Peace to tribes,
> Manifold sureties,
> True judgments,
> Fasting upon neighbouring territories,
> Exalting privileged persons,
> Honouring poets,
> Worshipping great God,

Fertility during his reign,

Taking cognizance of every wretch,

Many alms,

Mast upon trees,

Fish in river-mouths,

Earth fruitful,

Inviting barks into harbour,

Importing treasures from over sea,

Forfeiture of sea-waifs,

Silken raiment,

A sword-smiting troop to protect every
    tribe,

Raids across borders,

Let him attend to the sick,

Let him benefit the strong,

Let him possess truth,

Let him chide falsehood,

Let him love righteousness,

Let him beat down fear,

Let him crush criminals,

Let him give true judgments,
Let him foster every science,
Let him consolidate every peace,
Let him buy treasures,
Let him improve his soul,
Let him make known every clear
    judgment,
Abundance of wine and mead,
Let him utter every truth,
for it is through the truth of a ruler that God
gives all that.'

Ograndson of Conn, O Cormac,' said Carbre, 'what is the true right of a king?'

'Not hard to tell. The right that rules upon the surface of the earth, I have it, let me make it known to you,' said Cormac to Carbre.

> Let him restrain the great,
> Let him slay evildoers,
> Let him exalt the good,
> Let him put down robbers,
> Let him check theft,
> Let him adjust relationship,
> Let him consolidate peace,
> Let him plant law,
> Let him check unlawfulness,
> Let him enslave criminals,
> Let him set the innocent free,
> Let him protect the just,
> Let him bind the unjust,
> Let him proclaim robbers,—

Full forfeiture for every hand with fines,

Composition (?) with full fines where
there was knowledge, with half fines
where there was ignorance,

 With due respect for a king,

 With due exactions (?) for a lord,

 Let him perfect the proper due of every
    man, of whatever is his on sea and land,

 With just substances to the tribes which
    are his, for crimes of hand,

 Walking about of feet,

 Looking of eyes, for crimes of mouth,

 With hearing of ears,

 With tests of conscience,

 Let him study the right of every chief,

 Let him bring each one under law—
for those are the duties of a lord towards tribes.'

O grandson of Conn, O Cormac,' said Carbre, 'what is best for the good of a tribe?'

'Not hard to tell,' said Cormac.

> 'A meeting of nobles,
>
> Frequent assemblies,
>
> An enquiring mind,
>
> Questioning the wise,
>
> Quelling every evil,
>
> Fulfilling every good,
>
> An assembly according to rules,
>
> Following ancient lore,
>
> A lawful synod,
>
> A lawful lord,
>
> Righteous chieftains,
>
> Not to crush wretches,
>
> Keeping treaties,
>
> Mercifulness with good customs,
>
> Consolidating kinship,
>
> Weaving together synchronisms,

Fulfilling the law,

Legality of ancient alliances,

A covenant without curtailment,

Warrior-bands without overbearing,

Manliness against foes,

Honesty towards brothers,

Just sureties,

Full compensations,

Righteous judgments,

Honest witnesses,

Keeping a bargain without detriment,

Interest on detriment,

Evenly balanced substances,

Ready hiring,

Hostages for honour,

Lending without stint,

Acceptable loans,

An equivalent for every good,

A dignified response,

Legitimate measure,

Learning every art,

Knowledge of every language,

Skill in variegated work,

Pleading with established maxims,

Passing judgment with precedents,

Giving alms,

Mercy towards the poor,

Pledges for (carrying out) judgments,

Honest guarantees,

Listening to elders,

Turning a deaf ear to the rabble,

Guarding the frontier against every evil,

Let him not be smooth-faced where the
good of the tribe is concerned,

Let him not be greasy in the mead-court
house—

that is best for the good of a tribe.'

O grandson of Conn, O Cormac,' said Carbre, 'what are the dues of a chief and of an ale-house?'

'Not hard to tell,' said Cormac.

> 'Good behaviour around a good chief,
> Lights to lamps,
> Exerting oneself for the company,
> Settling seats,
> Liberality of dispensers,
> A nimble hand at distributing,
> Attentive service,
> To love one's lord,
> Music in moderation,
> Short story-telling,
> A joyous countenance,
> Welcome to companies,
> Silence during a recital (?),
> Harmonious choruses—

those are the dues of a chief and of an ale-house,' said Cormac to Carbre.

O grandson of Conn, O Cormac,' said Carbre, 'whence is chieftaincy taken over tribes, and clans, and races?'

'Not hard to tell,' said Cormac.

> 'By virtue of shape and race and knowledge, through wisdom and rank and liberality and honesty, by virtue of hereditary right and eloquence, by the strength of fighting and an army it is taken.'

Question, what are the proper qualities of a chief?' said Carbre.

'Not hard to tell,' said Cormac.

'Let him have good *gessa*,

let him be sober,

let him be an invader,

let him have good desires,

let him be affable,

let him be humble,

let him be proud,

let him be quick,

let him be steadfast,

let him be a poet,

let him be versed in legal lore.

let him be wise,

let him be generous,

let him be decorous,

let him be sociable,

let him be gentle,

let him be hard,

let him be loving,

let him be merciful,

let him be righteous,

let him be keen,

let him be persevering,

let him be patient,

let him be abstinent,

let him raise up the weak by the strong,

let him give true judgments,

let him feed every orphan,

let him quell every wrong (?),

let him hate falsehood,

let him love truth,

let him be forgetful of wrong,

let him be mindful of good,

let him be attended by a host
  in gatherings,

let him be attended by few in secret
  councils,

let him be brilliant in company,

let him be the sun of the mead-hall,

let him be an entertainer of a gathering
and assembly,

let him be a lover of knowledge and wisdom,

let him be a chastíser of wrong,

let him be masterful to check every one
that may be undutiful,

let him judge every one according to his
proper right,

let him give his due to each,

let him be a judge of every one according
to his rank,

let him be liberal to every one according
to their degree and profession,

let his covenants be firm,

let his levies be lenient,

let his judgments and decisions be sharp
and light,

for it is by those qualities kings and lords are
judged,' said Cormac to Carbre.

O grandson of Conn, O Cormac,' said Carbre, 'what were your habits when you were a lad?'

'Not hard to tell,' said Cormac.
> 'I was a listener in woods,
>
> I was a gazer at stars,
>
> I was blind where secrets were
>   concerned,
>
> I was silent in a wilderness,
>
> I was talkative among many,
>
> I was mild in the mead-hall,
>
> I was stern in battle,
>
> I was ready to watch,
>
> I was gentle in friendship,
>
> I was a physician of the sick,
>
> I was weak towards the strengthless,
>
> I was strong towards the powerful,
>
> I never was hard lest I be satirised,
>
> I never was feeble lest I should have my
>   hair stript off,

I was not close lest I should be
burdensome,

I was not arrogant though I was wise,

I was not given to promising though I
was strong,

I was not venturesome though I was
swift,

I did not deride old people though I was
young,

I was not boastful though I was a good
fighter,

I would not speak about anyone in his
absence,

I would not reproach, but I would praise,

I would not ask, but I would give,

for it is through those habits that the young
become old and kingly warriors.'

O grandson of Conn, O Cormac,' said Carbre, 'what were your deeds when you were a young man?'

'Not hard to tell,' said Cormac.

> 'I would slay a boar, I would follow a
> track when I was alone,
> I would march against a troop of five
> when I was one of five,
> I was ready to slay and wreck when I was
> one of ten,
> I was ready for a raid when I was one of
> twenty,
> I was ready to give battle when I was one
> of a hundred—

those were my deeds,' said Cormac to Carbre.

O grandson of Conn, O Cormac,' said Carbre, 'what do you deem the worst thing you have seen?'

'Not hard to tell,' said Cormac.
    'Faces of foes in a battle-field.'

O grandson of Conn, O Cormac,' said Carbre, 'what do you deem the sweetest thing you have heard?'

'Not hard to tell,' said Cormac.
    'A pæan after victory,
    Praise after wages,
    A lady's invitation to her pillow.'

O grandson of Conn, O Cormac,' said Carbre, 'what is best for me?'

'Not hard to tell,' said Cormac. 'If you listen to my teaching, do not give your honour for ale nor for food, for it is better to save one's fair fame than to save one's food.

>Be not proud unless you be a land-owner,
>do not keep bridled steeds without (a stud) of horses,
>do not give banquets without (brewing) ale,
>be not prodigal of dairy-produce without kine,
>do not dress elegantly unless you possess sheep,
>for pride without husbandry,
>luxury without horses,
>banqueting without ale,

dairy-produce without kine,
elegant dress without sheep
are a crime in the gatherings of the world.'

O grandson of Conn, O Cormac,' said Carbre, 'what is good for me?'

'Not hard to tell,' said Cormac. 'If you listen to my teaching,

> do not deride any old person though you
>   are young,
> nor a poor one though you are rich,
> nor a naked one though you are well-clad,
> nor a lame one though you are swift,
> nor a blind one though you are
>   keen-sighted,
> nor an invalid though you are strong,
> nor a dull one though you are clever,
> nor a fool though you are wise,
> be not slothful,
> be not fierce,
> be not sleepy,
> be not niggardly.

be not feckless,

be not jealous,

for every lazy, fierce, sleepy, niggardly, feckless, jealous person is hateful before God and men.'

O grandson of Conn, O Cormac,' said Carbre, 'how do you distinguish the race of Adam?'

'Not hard to tell,' said Cormac. 'I distinguish them all, both men, women, sons, and daughters.'

  'How is that?' said Carbre.

> 'Every steadfast person is wise,
> every generous person is righteous,
> every patient person is persevering,
> every studious person is learned,
> every one who loves his kindred is gentle,
> every healthy person is joyous,
> every sleek person is sleepy,
> every boor is crabbed,
> every athlete is dull-witted,
> every madcap is a laughing-stock,
> every serf is morose,
> every indigent person is proud,
> every uninformed person is quarrelsome,

every ignoramus is shameless,

every timorous person is apprehensive,

every infirm person is candid,

every ill-favoured person is given
   to fostering,

every anxious person is timid,

every timorous person is cautious,

every timid person is ruthless,

every indigent person is fraudulent,

every contentious person is a frequenter
   of meetings,

every satiated person is fond of dogs,

every lover likes a dainty bed,

every wealthy person is fond of jewels,

every freeman is broad-tracked,

every genial person is generous,

every satirical person is . . . ,

every horseman is nimble,

every falsehood is bitter,

everything true is sweet,

skilful women are honey-mouthed,
bad women are given to trysting,
ill-met are their sons, woe to him who
has them!'

O grandson of Conn, O Cormac,' said Carbre, 'and the ways of folly, what is their number?'

'Not hard to tell,' said Cormac.
'Swearing after judgment,
rash judgments,
rousing anger,
false (after-wise *DN*) grumbling,
chiding truth,
renouncing the prayer-house,
reversing judgments,
sorrow at a feast,
a lying chief,
laughter at an old man,
concealing ancient lore,
playing upon a cliff,
a cast without a proper grip,
competing with a fool,
being haughty with a king,
not to fulfil the law,

to fulfil whatever is evil,

(to harbour) evil against an ally,

to keep company with every one,

to hold any new thing fair,

to hold everything familiar an enemy,

to act without a witness,

being a feeble master,

buying judgments,

to be without treasures,

much lending,

many friends,

sorrow in the presence of a king,

talking much without wisdom,—

that is the way of folly,' said Cormac.

Knowledge deserves to be honoured,

wisdom vanquishes valour,

every timid person is opinionate,

every lover is melancholy,

every sick person is . . . ,

every liar is quarrelsome,

every fool is dangerous,

every arrogant person runs a risk,

every fierce person is ready to strike,

every farmer is prudent,

every bad warrior is violent,

every person with vested interests
   is shameless,

every timorous person is easily
   frightened,

everything dark is awful, every plebeian
   is low,

whoever is fond of ease is corpulent,

every unfortunate person is vehement.

every guilty person is apprehensive,

every reviler is precipitate,

every cautious person is timorous,

every foulmouthed person is quarrelsome,

every one fond of company is brilliant,

every brave tribe is fond of gatherings,

every brave king holds encampments,

every aggressor is puissant,

every bold person is cheerful,

every big talker is neglectful,

every one making promises readily
is false,

every lavish person is overweening,

every hasty person is ridiculous,

every powerful person is liable to
be reviled,

every reviler is stubborn,

every sensible person is competent.

O grandson of Conn, O Cormac,' said Carbre, 'how do you distinguish weathers?'

'Not hard to tell,' said Cormac.
> 'Ice is the mother of corn,
> snow is the father of fat,
> a shower is a presage of bloodshed,
> drought is a presage of pestilence,
> wind is most troublesome in a strait,
> the best of weathers is mist,
> better his brother rain,
> save for the sea, thunder is not fruitful.'

O grandson of Conn, O Cormac,' said Carbre, 'what is the worst housekeeping?'

'Not hard to tell. A housekeeping by which neither honour nor life is bought. There is another housekeeping which is worse:

'Get, fetch, take, bring!'

I tem Cormac ad Carbre:

      'Do not contend with a king,
      do not forgather with a fool,
      do not associate with a marauder,
      do not fraternize with an evil-doer,
   do not buy from the seven imbeciles
according to the law of the Irish, viz. from a
woman, from a caitiff, from a drunken person,
from a buffoon, from a madman, from a
superior, from a . . . ,
   do not race against a wheel, nor against
the cast of a spear, nor up a great height, nor
against the surf of the sea, nor against danger,
nor a lance,
      do not join in blasphemy,
      be not the laughing-stock of an assembly,
      be not sorrowful in an alehouse,
      be not forgetful of an assignation.
      do not be indocile,

do not be a wrangler against truth,

take no cognizance of falsehood,

do not be the servant of robbers,

do not be a leader in strife,

do not be a bush of discord,

do not lend your lips to every one,

do not promise what you have not,

be not fond of buying lest you be
     encumbered by debts,

be no fighter lest you be disgraced,

be not contentious lest you be hateful,

be no wrangler lest you get your
     head broken,

be not rough lest you become ungainly,

be not quarrelsome lest you be . . . ,

be not an absentee lest you become
     negligent,

be not hard lest you become churlish,

be not too generous lest you be left
     stranded,

be not lazy lest you become enfeebled,

do not bustle too much lest you
become vile,

be not cantankerous lest you become
unsociable,

do not become a guarantor for any one
lest your neighbour . . .'

O grandson of Conn, O Cormac,' said Carbre,
'what is most lasting on earth?'

'Not hard to tell,' said Cormac. 'Grass, copper,
a yew-tree.'

O grandson of Conn, O Cormac,' said Carbre, 'what is the worst for the body of man?'

'Not hard to tell,' said Cormac. 'Sitting too long, lying too long, long standing, heavy lifts, exertions beyond one's strength, . . . , running too much, leaping too much, frequent falls, sleeping with one's leg over the bedrail, swift racing, gazing at glowing embers, stepping in the dark, wax, beestings, new ale, bull-flesh, curdles, dry food, bog-water, rising too early, cold, sun, hunger, drinking too much, eating too much, sleeping too much, sinning too much, grief, running up a height, shouting against the wind, a blow beyond one's strength, drying oneself by a fire, summer-dew, winter-dew, beating ashes, swimming on a full stomach, sleeping on one's back, a deep drink, frenzy, foolish romping.'

O grandson of Conn, O Cormac,' said Carbre, 'what is the worst pleading and arguing?'

'Not hard to tell,' said Cormac. 'Seventeen signs of bad pleading, viz.:

>Contending against knowledge,
>
>taking refuge in bad language,
>
>much abuse,
>
>contending without proofs,
>
>stiffness of delivery,
>
>a muttering speech,
>
>hair-splitting,
>
>uncertain proofs,
>
>despising books,
>
>turning against customs,
>
>talking in too loud a voice,
>
>shifting one's pleading,
>
>inciting the multitude,
>
>fighting everybody,

blowing one's own trumpet,
shouting at the top of one's voice,
swearing after judgment.'

O grandson of Conn, O Cormac,' said Carbre,
'what is the worst pleading?'

'Not hard to tell,' said Cormac. 'A rash forgetful
pleading.'

O grandson of Conn, O Cormac,' said Carbre, 'what is the worst arguing?'

'Not hard to tell,' said Cormac. 'An argument based on oaths, a feeble, slow, stiff argument.'

O grandson of Conn, O Cormac,' said Carbre,
'what is the worst arguing before an assembly?'

'Not hard to tell,' said Cormac.
　　　'A violent, stubborn, long-winded
　　　　　arguing,
　　　an unsteady arguing,
　　　a hollow loose suing,
　　　a vehement oblivious pleading,
　　　rousing anger,
　　　very violent urging,
　　　playing a dangerous game,
　　　rash reckless oaths,
　　　a loud open-mouthed answer,
　　　to disconcert the meeting,
　　　slanderous words,
　　　hand . . .'

O grandson of Conn, O Cormac,' said Carbre, 'what is the worst pleading?'

'Not hard to tell,' said Cormac.

> 'A pleading without instruction,
>> without knowledge,
> violence in discussion,
> discussion without reason,
> a pleading without choice,
>> without restraint, without grasp,
>> without practice.'

O grandson of Conn, O Cormac,' said Carbre, 'who are the worst for whom you have a comparison?'

'Not hard to tell,' said Cormac.
> 'A man with the impudence of a satirist,
> with the pugnacity of a slave-woman,
> with the carelessness of a . . . dog,
> with the conscience of a hound,
> with a robber's hand,
> with a bull's strength,
> with the dignity of a judge,
> with keen ingenious wisdom,
> with the speech of a stately man,
> with the memory of an historian,
> with the behaviour of an abbot,
> with the swearing of a horse-thief,

and he wise, lying, grey-haired, violent, swearing, garrulous when he says 'the matter is settled, I swear, I shall swear.'

O grandson of Conn, O Cormac,' said Carbre, 'who are the worst for whom you further have a comparison?'

'Not hard to tell,' said Cormac. 'A rough, bitter, rude, violent, vehement, vulgar, impetuous, forgetful, noisy, impudent, after-wise man, to whom no one attends, who does not attend to any one, who does not care what anyone else says, while no one cares what he says, and he proscribed both by the laity and by the Church.'

O grandson of Conn, O Cormac,' said Carbre,
'I desire to know how I shall behave among
the wise and the foolish, among friends and
strangers, among the old and the young, among
the innocent and the wicked.'

'Not hard to tell,' said Cormac.

> 'Be not too wise, be not too foolish,
> be not too conceited, be not too diffident,
> be not too haughty, be not too humble,
> be not too talkative, be not too silent,
> be not too harsh, be not too feeble.
> If you be too wise, one will expect (too
> much) of you;
> if you be too foolish, you will be deceived;
> if you be too conceited, you will be thought
> vexatious;
> if you be too humble, you will be without
> honour;

if you be too talkative, you will not
be heeded;
if you be too silent, you will not
be regarded;
if you be too harsh, you will be broken;
if you be too feeble, you will be crushed.'

A question,' said Carbre, 'how shall I be?'

'Not hard to tell,' said Cormac.
　　　'Be wise with the wise lest anyone
　　　　　deceive you in wisdom,
　　　be proud with the proud lest anyone
　　　　　make you tremble.
　　　be humble with the humble when your
　　　　　will is being done,
　　　be talkative with the talkative . . . .
　　　be silent with the silent when a recital is
　　　　　being listened to,
　　　be hard with the hard lest anyone
　　　　　slight you,
　　　be gentle with the gentle lest everyone
　　　　　. . . you.'

Cormac further has said this:

'Every one is wise till he comes to sell
   his heritage,
every one is foolish till he buys land,
every one is a friend till it comes to debts,
every one is a law-giver till it comes
   to children,
every one is sleepy till it comes
   to marrying,
every one is ferocious till it comes
   to piety,
every one is fair-famed till he is satirised,
every one is a hospitaller till he refuses
   (to entertain),
every one is a roving warrior till he takes
   up husbandry,
every one is a mercenary till he settles in
   a dwelling,

every one is *compos mentis* till he becomes
   drunk,
every one is reasonable till he gets angry,
every one is decorous till he commits
   adultery,
every one is tranquil till he has
   foster-children,
every one is a counsellor till he begins
   to quarrel,
every one is a citizen till he is
   proclaimed,
every one is joyful till he meets with
   ill-luck,
every one is bold till he meets with
   a refusal,
every one is a pedestrian till he drives
   a chariot,
all music is holy till it comes to the harp,
every fortunate creature is fair,

every unfortunate creature is foul,
the sweetest part of sleep is cohabitation,
the sweetest part of ale is the
    first draught,
music is sweetest in the dark,
the sweetest part of a meal is the
    honorific portion.
A docile, humble, obedient young man of a nice
conscience and confession, his youth will be
lovable, his old age venerable, his word will
be true, his countenance will be chaste, he
will be exalted though low, he will be old though
young, his end will be good with God and man.'

O grandson of Conn, O Cormac,' said Carbre, 'what is the code of ridicule among the Irish?'

'Not hard to tell,' said Cormac.

> 'A man proud of his wisdom, his gifts,
>   his good fortune,
> fastidious, standing on his dignity,
>   vainglorious,
> a lazy, violent, feeble, flighty man,
> a silly, dull, big-worded man,
> a wrathful, aggressive, masterful man,
> a man niggardly, unstable, jealous, . . .
>   timorous, violent, impulsive,
>   incautious, loveless, . . .
>   tedious, angry.

O grandson of Conn, O Cormac,' said Carbre, 'who is the worst guarantor?'

'Not hard to tell,' said Cormac. 'A black-mouthed guarantor of small honour, who sells his cheek and his knee and his hand and his breast and his heart and the honour of his children and of his race and his valour.

His amends are barren,
his honour-price is hollow,
his character is changeable (?),
his . . . is short,
his protection is narrow,
his arm is not smaller than his dignity,
his figure is a pattern of mockery in the sight of all men,
he is a hang-head butt of ridicule wherever he go or be.

O son, if you listen to me,' said Cormac, 'this is my instruction to you:

> Do not let a man with friends be your
>   steward,
> nor a woman with sons and fostersons
>   your housekeeper,
> nor a man of many desires your dispenser,
> nor a man of much delay your miller,
> nor a violent foul-mouthed man your
>   messenger,
> nor a grumbling sluggard your servant,
> nor a garrulous man your counsellor,
> nor a bibulous man your cup-bearer,
> nor a man with a bad sight your watchman,
> nor a bitter, haughty man your doorkeeper,
> nor a compassionate man your judge,
> nor a man without knowledge your leader,
> nor an unfortunate man your adviser.'

O grandson of Conn, whom do you deem the deafest you have heard?'

'Not hard to tell. A fey person who is being warned,

    one who is asked what he does not like,

    the tattle of a silly woman.'

O grandson of Conn, what are the best seasons?'

'Not hard to tell. A fine frosty winter,

    a dry windy spring,

    a droughty showery summer,

    a fruitful autumn with heavy dews.'

O grandson of Conn, what do you think the worst you have heard?'

'Not hard to tell. An outcry after outrage,
　　　the groan of disease,
　　　a womanish quarrel between two men.'